Larry Burkett's

Faith Kids® is an imprint of Cook Communications Ministries,
Colorado Springs, Colorado 80918
Cook Communications, Paris, Ontario
Kingsway Communications, Eastbourne, England

MONEY PLANNER FOR KIDS
© 2001 by Burkett & Kids, LLC

First printing, 2001
Printed in the United States.
1 2 3 4 5 6 7 8 9 10 Printing/Year 05 04 03 02 01

Editor: Heather Gemmen
Designer: Keith Sherrer of iDesignEtc.

Larry Burkett's

MONEY PLANNER for KIDS

LIGHTwave
building Christian faith in families

Equipping Kids for Life
faithkids.com

CONTENTS

INTRODUCTION

The sun beat down on Jordan and his sister Amanda as they stood staring up at the huge, old cherry tree that stood majestically in their backyard.

"Our tree house has got to be two stories high with bunk beds upstairs for sleep-overs," Amanda said.

"Oh yeah," Jordan responded. "And we need a crow's-nest lookout, a secret compartment to hide in . . . and a rope ladder!"

Amanda grinned. "Don't forget the water balloon launcher and locking trapdoor."

"Hey!" Jordan turned to his sister. "Let's quit dreaming and just do it. Mom and Dad said we're allowed, and we know how. What are we waiting for?"

So they grabbed their younger brother's wagon, headed off to Bob's Build It Center, and bought some nails and boards for the first platform. Then they went home and started building.

After a few days (and a little advice from Dad) the children completed the first platform. It was strong and perfectly square. Jordan and Amanda were so pleased with themselves that they rushed back to buy more supplies. But when they got to Bob's and put their money together, they realized they had made a terrible mistake: they had spent so much money perfecting the first platform that they did not have enough money left to complete the walls—never mind the second story, the roof, or any of their other dream features.

"We should have done this before we even

started," grumbled Jordan as he and his sister sat down outside the store and tried to figure out how much it would cost to build the rest of their tree house. They could hardly believe their eyes.

"Three hundred and sixty-five dollars!" Amanda exploded. "There's no way."

"We won't be able to do the second story or the balloon launcher or ... well, just about anything else," groaned Jordan. "We need a way to get more money."

The children dragged their feet as they walked home. They wished they had never told their friends about their dream tree house. Now they would have to put up with teasing every time their friends passed by the tree platform.

What do you think Jordan and Amanda should have done differently? Would everything have turned out okay if they just had enough money? Not necessarily. If they had spent all their money on the tree house, what would they have used for summer spending, camp, and even junk food for the summer sleep-overs?

Anyone who has done well with money will tell you that the secret to financial success is not how much money you make, but how well you manage it. Some professional athletes, who are great at sports but don't know how to manage their money, make millions of dollars and still retire with nothing. But if you start saving and investing just one dollar per day, you would retire with close to one million dollars in the bank. Managing your money isn't just saving and investing. It's planning and applying God's money principles to earning, giving, and spending as well.

Jesus told us that everything we have is a gift from God. This includes our time, talents, and our treasures. As the keepers of God's gifts, we don't own anything at all. All we do is manage things for God. Jesus wants us to become good stewards, or managers, of the things God gives us (Matthew 25:15–30). Money Planner for Kids will help you keep track of the treasures God gives you so that you can become the good and faithful steward he wants you to be.

This book is divided into four chapters according to the four things you can do with money—earn it, give it, save it, and spend it. Each chapter includes a short introduction with great tips on how to manage your money followed by a bunch of easy and fun pages to help you do it well. Read each introduction carefully. Then read through the pages that follow to make sure you understand them. Get some help from your parents or older siblings if you need it. Once you have a good handle on things, start using the worksheets to help you keep track of how you use your money. You'll be amazed at how easy and rewarding good stewardship is if you plan ahead.

CHAPTER ONE

Earning

If I offer you two dollars to wash my car and you agree, what have we just done? We've made a deal. You have just agreed to exchange some of your time and talent for some of my money. That's what earning is all about. You may also receive allowance for doing household chores or for simply being part of the family.

To help you plan your earning goals, you'll want to ask yourself a number of key questions. **The first is,** where can I find a job? At your age, most of the jobs you are qualified for can be found at home, in your neighborhood, or with your friends or extended family. These include things like household chores, yard work, paper delivery routes, dog walking, and so on. Keep your eyes and ears open to see what is available. Ask your parents, family friends, and relatives if they need some extra help. Tell them you are looking for a way to earn money.

The second question you should try to answer before you even start your job hunt is, what are my skills—that is, what am I good at? Are you an experienced raker? Have you ever done any painting? Are you good with animals? How are your sweeping skills? Learn how to make a resume (see page 14) that you can present to possible employers. Then you will know which jobs you are able to do and which you are not.

The third question you need to ask yourself is, how much is my time is worth? A potential employer will ask how much you want to be paid to do the job. You figure this out by checking around for the "going rate" for different jobs. For example, if most kids in the neighborhood are willing to rake leaves for two dollars an hour, chances are no employer is going to pay you five dollars an hour to do it—even though you think you're worth it. Be reasonable, check out the going rates, then make your decision. And remember, you might not get paid what you want right away. Part of your job is to prove that you deserve to be paid well because you work hard and do a good job.

> *The two basic ways to be paid for a job are by the hour or by the task.* *If you get paid by the hour, you can be sure that you are paid for every hour you work; but if you work too slow, your employer will likely not hire you again. If you get paid by the job, you might finish sooner or later than you planned, giving you a higher or lower wage. Your employer will usually decide how you will be paid, but make sure that it is a good deal for both of you.*

The fourth thing you'll want to ask yourself is, how much time do I have available for working. You probably spend most of your day at school, so your work time is limited to after school hours and weekends. You also have home-work, lessons, church, clubs, sports, and regular chores to take into account. Use the Time Budgeter (on page 17) to help you figure out how much time you have available each week.

Finally, before you take on a job, you need to make sure that your attitude is in the right place. When you do a job, do your best so that you can feel proud of what you've done and your employer is happy with your work. The Bible says, "Whatever you do, work at it with all your heart, as working for the Lord, not for men" (Colossians 3:23). That means whenever you do a job, you're not just doing it for the person who hired you, you're doing it for God.

Therefore, no matter who you're working for, you only ever have one boss: God. And he always wants you to do your best.

Jordan and Amanda

When Jordan and Amanda realized how much

their dream tree house was going to cost them, they got discouraged and thought they would have to scale back their plans or quit the project altogether. But after talking to their parents, they realized that maybe they could still reach their goal if they took on part-time jobs and earned some money. So they each created a resume, figured out how many hours they had available for working each week, then went on a job hunt. By the end of the week, Jordan had a regular job weeding the neighbor lady's flower beds and Amanda got a paper route. They became excited about their project again.

Tools

1. Your Resume

In this chapter you learned that you need to figure out what your skills and training are and what sort of work they qualify you to do. A resume is a list of all of your skills and training that you can give to someone when applying for a job. Photocopy the simple resume form (on page 16) and fill it out.

The **Personal Information** section provides potential employers with your name and how to contact you. The **Education** section gives them an idea of how old you are and where you go to school. **The Jobs I Can Do for You** section should include three jobs that you would like to do and would be good at. The **Work Experience** section is where you list any other jobs you've done that you have been paid for (whether for your parents or for someone else). Put your most recent job first. The **Skills and Abilities** section should include any skills you've learned at home, at school, or through other tasks that would be helpful in the job you are applying for. Finally, the **References** section should include the names, addresses, and telephone numbers of three people for whom you have worked.

Once you're finished, ask your parents to photo-copy the completed form or type up the information on your computer so you can hand out a copy of your resume whenever you apply for a job.

2. Time Budgeter

The time budgeting worksheet (on page 17) will help you figure out how much time you have available for work each week. Photocopy the form as many times as you want. In the spaces provided, write down what you do dur-ing every hour of the day in a typical week. This includes activities like school, homework, household chores, sports practices, and so on. Tally up your available work hours at the bottom of the form to see the total number of hours you have available for work each week. This will give you a general idea of how much or how little work you need to find. If you don't have many hours available, perhaps you will need to cut back on something in order to free up more time.

MY RESUME

PERSONAL INFORMATION
Name:_____ Age:_____
Address:_____
Phone:_____

EDUCATION
Name of school:_____
Grade completed:_____

JOBS I CAN DO FOR YOU
1._____
2._____
3._____

WORK EXPERIENCE
1. Job I did:_____
Employer:_____
When I did it:_____

2. Job I did:_____
Employer:_____
When I did it:_____

SKILLS AND ABILITIES
1._____
2._____
3._____

REFERENCES
1. Name:_____
Address:_____
Phone:_____

2. Name:_____
Address:_____
Phone:_____

WEEKLY SCHEDULE

	Monday	Tuesday	Wednesday	Thursday	Friday	Saturday	Sunday
8:00							
9:00							
10:00							
11:00							
12:00							
1:00							
2:00							
3:00							
4:00							
5:00							
6:00							
7:00							
8:00							
9:00							
10:00							
Hours Avail.:							

TOTAL: _____ hrs/wk

CHAPTER TWO

Giving

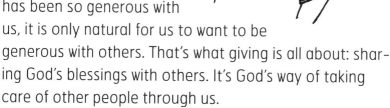

If someone does something nice for you, what's the first thing you want to do for them or someone else? Something nice in return, of course. God did something very generous for us by putting us in charge of some of his things. Whatever we have, it is a gift from God that he has freely given to us. Once we see how God has been so generous with us, it is only natural for us to want to be generous with others. That's what giving is all about: sharing God's blessings with others. It's God's way of taking care of other people through us.

We all have needs and wants. Needs are things that we cannot do without—things like food, water, and clothing. Wants are things that we only think we can't do without—things like ice cream, video games, and designer clothes. Giving is all about doing without some of our wants, and maybe even a few of our needs, to help others. For this reason, giving is not easy. It involves sacrifice. You may worry that if you give away some of your money you'll never have enough to buy the things you want and need. But God's kingdom doesn't work that way. In fact, it works exactly the opposite. "Remember this: Whoever sows sparingly will also reap sparingly, and whoever sows generously will also reap generously" (2 Corinthians 9:6). The key is trusting God to take care of you just like he says he will.

Giving doesn't just help others, it also helps the person who gives. For one thing, it helps us to become more like God. Generosity is part of God's nature. Giving also helps us to become more focused on the things God cares about and to value the things he values. Our focus shouldn't be on only money and possessions, but on people, relationships, and obedience to God. "For where your treasure is, there your heart will be also" (Luke 12:34).

So, we know giving is a good thing to do. But how do we do it? Who do we give to? And how much? In the Old Testament, the Israelites were to give God 10 percent (a tithe) of everything they grew or earned (e.g. one dime for every dollar) to thank God for all that he had given them. Today we aren't under the same law as the Israelites, but the tithe is still a good starting point for our giving efforts. Giving God the first of what we earn is a wise idea because if we wait until we've used our money to meet all of our wants and needs, there probably won't be much left for giving to others. Most people give their tithe to their church. This money helps pay for the church building, the pastor's salary, missionaries that the church supports, and so on. It's part of God's plan for how his work gets done.

But you don't have to stop your giving at 10 per-cent of your earnings. The tithe is just a starting point. You can give extra money to charities and missionaries, adopt a poor child from overseas, or help a friend at school who is less fortunate than you. You don't have to look far to find someone in need. You can't help everyone, but you can make a huge difference in the lives of a few people.

How often should you give? Most people tithe every week at church. Other people tithe at the beginning of every month. Talk with your parents and go with a schedule that works for you. Use the worksheet on page 25 to help you come up with a giving plan. As you work through the worksheet, remember all that God has given to you. Once you catch the heart of it, giv-ing can be a lot of fun. That's great, because God loves a cheerful giver (2

Corinthians 9:7). Never think that the little you do doesn't make a big difference in the world. God has a way of mak-ing mountains out of mole hills. Just you wait and see!

Jordan and Amanda

Jordan and Amanda heard a presentation in their church about the work a missionary was doing to help the poor in South America. After talking with their parents and filling out the giving goal form below, they each decided to give 10 percent of their earnings to their church.

"Let's give a little extra to help the missionary in South America," Amanda suggested. "It will take us longer to save up for the tree house, but the money we're earning is really a gift from God anyway."

"And it is important to share with others," agreed Jordan. "Besides, it feels good to know that we're helping to make other people's lives better."

Tools

1. Giving Goals Form

You have many opportunities to give money to help others—around the world or right in your backyard. You are only working with a small amount of money, so you can't give to everyone. Therefore, part of your job as a giver is to plan how much to give and to whom.

Photocopy the form on page 25 and answer the questions to help you come up with your own list of giving goals.

MY GIVING PLANNER

Your church's name:_____

How often would you like to give to your church? (check one)
 ❏ Weekly ❏ Monthly

How much would you like to give?
 $_____ per week $_____ per month

Does your church have any special offerings or missionary offerings?
 ❏ No ❏ Yes_____

How often would you like to give to the special offering? (check one)
 ❏ Weekly ❏ Monthly

How much would you like to give?
 $_____ per week $_____ per month

Does your family support a local charity or ministry you can help with?
If so, which one?_____

_____

What do they do?_____

_____

How often would you like to give to the local ministry? (check one)
 ❏ Weekly ❏ Monthly

How much would you like to give?
 $_____ per week $_____ per month

CHAPTER THREE

Saving

Have you ever walked into a bicycle store and drooled over all of the cool mountain bikes for sale—full suspension, hydraulic brakes, smooth shifters, and awesome paint jobs? Then you look at the price tags. Yikes, how could anyone ever afford something like that? To tell you the truth, most people can't afford to buy things like mountain bikes all at once; they have to save towards the things they want. By putting away a little money each week or each month, eventually they are able to afford it.

Saving is putting aside a planned amount of money each week or each month so that one day you will have enough to buy the things that cost more than you have to spend in one week or month. But we don't just save for things we want, such as mountain bikes. We also save for things we need, for helping others when they are in need, and for some of life's little surprises (such as when we accidentally throw a baseball through a window and have to pay for the repairs).

Saving is God's plan to help us prepare for the future. By planning ahead, we can be ready for whatever life brings our way. It's all part of being wise. As the Bible says, "In the house of the wise are stores of choice food and oil, but a foolish man devours all he has" (Proverbs 21:20). But we don't save money just so we can build up a pile of cash. That's called hoarding. When we hoard money, we are saying that we don't trust God to take care of us. We are trusting in money instead. We should always save for a purpose, not merely to grow rich.

So how do you start saving? The first thing you need to do is come up with some savings goals. These can be divided into two types: short-term and long-term savings. Short-term savings goals can be reached within weeks or a couple of months. These might include things like new shoes or a special giving project for your church. Long-term savings goals are those that will take more than two months to reach. These might include things like a scooter or a microscope.

How do you reach these goals? Whether they are short-term or long-term all of your savings goals can be reached the same way: one step at a time. Little by little, day by day, month by month, you set aside a certain amount towards these goals. A good rule of thumb is to commit the first 10 percent of your earnings to your tithe, 25 percent to short-term savings, 25 percent to long-term savings, and 40 percent to general spending. By the way, any bills, debts, or payments you owe should come out of your 40 percent general spending. The Budget Tracker at the end of this book will help you do this.

Once you start saving money, you're going to need a place to put it. One place is My Giving Bank (available through Christian Financial Concepts), which divides your money into the different budgeting categories listed above. Or you could divide up your money into the various budget categories and store it in separate containers or envelopes. You may also want to talk to your parents about starting a bank account. (The cool thing about a bank account is that the bank will pay you to deposit your money with them.)

Saving money isn't easy, especially when there are so many things out there that you need and want. But the first time that you reach a savings goal and buy that thing you thought you could never afford, you'll know it's worth it. So start saving today!

Jordan and Amanda

Jordan and Amanda had been working hard and saving their money.

"Cool!" Amanda exclaimed after they had they calculated the cost of the roof and walls for the second floor. "Now we'll be able to go in the tree house even when it rains."

"Come on, let's go to Bob's and buy the materials. It should be about $100."

"Our next short-term savings goal should be the materials for the second story," Amanda suggested as they walked toward the hardware store. "Maybe we can even get it done before winter."

"Yeah, and we can make our long-term savings goal all the cool extra stuff. We should be able to save up another $160 for that over the winter. By next spring, we'll have our dream tree house."

Amanda and Jordan high-fived each other as they walked into Bob's.

Tools
1. Savings Planner

Photocopy the worksheet on page 33 and use it to help you decide your short-term and long-term savings goals. Once you reach a goal, scratch it off your list and start on a new one.

MY SAVINGS PLANNER

What are some things that you would like to save for?

1) _____

2) _____

3) _____

4) _____

5) _____

6) _____

Which of these items are short-term goals?

1) _____

2) _____

3) _____

Which of these items are long-term goals?

1) _____

2) _____

3) _____

Which short-term goal would you like to save for first?

_____

How much will you save per week?_____ Per month?_____

How long will it take you to reach your goal?_____

_____

Which long-term goal would you like to save for first?

_____

How much will you save per week?_____ Per month?_____

How long will it take you to reach your goal? _____

CHAPTER FOUR

Spending

Well, you've worked hard to earn your money (Good job!), you've given the first part to God (Way to go!), and you've come up with a budget to help you plan what to do with your money (Congratulations!). Now it's time to go out and paint the town red. Or is it? Is there more to spending than just running around willy-nilly buying the first thing that catches your fancy? You bet there is. Spending takes as much wisdom as every other stage of money management we've looked at so far. So it's worth your while to learn a bit about spending before you go out and do it.

Before we start looking at how you should spend your money, it's important to understand what spending is. Spending is the opposite of earning. Instead of money coming in, it's money going out. Spending is using your money to get the things you want and need, either for yourself or others.

Earlier on we talked about how your money should be split up. The 40 percent general spending is for things like birthday cards, snacks, little books, renting a video, and so on. But first make sure to cover your responsibilities (for instance, an overdue library fine). And remember, don't go out and spend all your money at once. Make it last.

> *It's no fun to pay off debts; but you racked up the bill, so you're responsible to pay it off. God wants us to be responsible in these matters so other people don't have to pay for our mistakes and so that we can model God's characteristics of faithfulness and trustworthiness to others.*

Now let's talk about bigger spending: buying the things you've saved for. Say you're shopping for a new personal CD player. How are you going to figure out which is the best brand to buy or what store will give you the most value for your money? Should you go for the cheapest CD player you can find or should you pay a little more to get an extra feature or a longer warranty. Come to think of it, what features do you want in a CD player anyway? The only way to find answers to these questions is through research. This means sifting through flyers, visiting or calling stores, comparing prices, and reading product reviews to see what other people say about different brands of CD players. You may need your parents to help you with this. The worksheets at the end of this chapter will help you as well. Whenever you go to spend your money, think about how hard you worked to earn it. This will make you want to get most for your money.

Once you've figured out which CD player you want, find the best place to buy it. Why pay $150 for a CD player at one store when you can get the same item at another store for $130? It pays to shop around. Check out at least three stores for every major item you buy. And ask the sales clerks when the item will go on sale. If you can wait until that happens, you will save even more money.

Here are three things to remember whenever you are thinking about spending some money: One, no matter how pressured you feel or how badly you want something, if it is not exactly what you want, don't buy it. Wait. Then wait some more. If you buy something in a hurry or out of excitement, you may regret it later. Two, always try to get the best value for your money. This doesn't always mean getting the cheapest thing you can find. Things are often cheap because they are of poor quality. If you're going to buy something, make sure you get the best item within your price range. Finally, make a spending plan and stick to it. There will be many temptations to leave your budget behind and go on a wild spending spree. Don't fall for it. It may look good at first, but you'll regret it in the end when you have nothing left to buy the things you really want or need.

CD Players

Now you know a bit about wise spending.

But before you go to town, work through the worksheet on page 43 and make sure your plan is solidly in place. Then stick to it. As Jesus said, "Wisdom is proved right by her actions" (Matthew 11:19). So go out there and show the world how wise you are!

Jordan and Amanda

Jordan and Amanda browsed through Bob's and noticed that some items in the store were on sale.

"I wish the things we wanted were on sale," Amanda moaned.

"Hey! Maybe some of this stuff is on sale at that home improvement store Dad goes to."

"Yeah, or maybe their regular prices are cheaper."

So Jordan and Amanda went home and did some research. With their wise-shopper checklists in hand, they set out in search of the best possible price for wood, nails, windows, and other materials they would need. They called a bunch of home

improvement stores, collected store coupons, and even looked through the classified ads for used building supplies. It took them a couple of weeks, but when they were finished, they found the materials they needed at a much cheaper price than they originally expected.

"Awesome," Jordan cheered as he and Amanda returned their dad's aluminum ladder to the garage. "I never expected to have enough money to pay for the rope ladder already."

"Dad might be disappointed, though. Now he has no excuse to avoid cleaning out the eaves troughs," Amanda giggled.

Tools

1. Wise-Shopper Checklist

It takes research to make sure you get the best value for your money. The worksheet on page 43 will help make the job easier by giving you a place to record your findings. It will allow you to compare cost, features, and quality among a variety of products so that it will be easier for you to make a wise spending choice. Photocopy and use it as many times as you want. And remember: Don't wait to start researching until you have all the money you need. Research while you're saving. You'll be more patient and will do a more thorough job.

WISE-SHOPPER CHECKLIST

PRODUCT INFORMATION

Item: _____ Desired Price: $ _____

Desired Features (from most important to least important):

1) _____ 4) _____

2) _____ 5) _____

3) _____ 6) _____

Brands/models that offer these features:

1) _____

Average Price: $ _____ (New) $ _____ (Used) $ _____

Features (From above. Check all that apply): ❏1 ❏2 ❏3 ❏4 ❏5 ❏6

Other Features: _____

Warranty? (Check one) ❏ Yes ❏ No How Long? _____ Cost? $ _____

2) _____

Average Price: $ _____ (New) $ _____ (Used) $ _____

Features (From above. Check all that apply): ❏1 ❏2 ❏3 ❏4 ❏5 ❏6

Other Features: _____

Warranty? (Check one) ❏ Yes ❏ No How Long? _____ Cost? $ _____

3) _____

Average Price: $ _____ (New) $ _____ (Used) $ _____

Features (From above. Check all that apply): ❏1 ❏2 ❏3 ❏4 ❏5 ❏6

Other Features: _____

Warranty? (Check one) ❏ Yes ❏ No How Long? _____ Cost? $ _____

STORE INFORMATION

1) Store name: _____

Phone number: _____ Price: $ _____

Sale coming up? (Check one) ❏ Yes ❏ No When? _____

2) Store name: _____

Phone number: _____ Price: $ _____

Sale coming up? (Check one) ❏ Yes ❏ No When? _____

3) Store name: _____

Phone number: _____ Price: $ _____

Sale coming up? (Check one) ❏ Yes ❏ No When? _____

CONCLUSION

Best product: _____ Place to buy: _____

Best price: _____ Best time to buy: _____

Jordan and Amanda

Jordan and Amanda reached their savings goals and purchased the building materials for their tree house in the early fall and began construction on the second story. With help from their parents, they were able to complete it before winter. They even got to spend a night in it before the snow came.

"By next spring it will be the most amazing tree house ever!" Jordan announced.

"If we stick to our plan and continue saving towards our goals, that is," Amanda reminded.

"Of course we will," Jordan replied happily. "Careful planning pays off. Not only do we have our dream tree house, we also have been able to give money to the poor and we almost always had enough money to afford to go to fun events this summer."

"And hasn't this been the best summer we ever had?" sighed Amanda dreamily.

BUDGET TRACKER

Every time you earn money for doing a job, deposit it in your account and divide it up into the categories on the Budget Tracker. Here's an example of how it works: On May 4th you earn $10.00 for raking leaves. The first thing you do is write the date in the left-hand column of the Budget Tracker. Then you divide the money you earned into the various categories starting with 10 percent ($1.00) into your giving account, 25 percent ($2.50) into short-term savings, 25 percent ($2.50) into long-term savings, and 40 percent ($4.00) into your spending account. Record each of these transactions as "deposits" in the Transactions column and put the amount of each deposit in the Balance column. If you already have money in your account or envelopes, simply add the amount you are depositing to what is already there and record the total in the Balance column.

When you want to take money out, record the amount you withdraw in the Transaction column and adjust the balance in that account. You might want to write what the withdrawal is for or simply record the fact that you took money out. When you reach a savings goal, empty that account, enter a new savings goal, and start over. Also, whenever you deposit or withdraw money from you accounts, make sure you update the Total All Balances column on the right side of the chart so you can keep track of how much money you have in total.

Good money planning worked for Jordan and Amanda. They worked and planned hard—and they enjoyed the process. With God's help, there's no reason why it can't work just as well for you. Have fun! ◣

(Budget Tracker from p. 190-191 in *Financial Parenting, 2nd Edition*)

MINI BUDGET

Date	GIVING / TITHING (10%)		SHORT-TERM SAVINGS	
	Transaction	Balance	Goal:	Co
			Transaction	

TRACKER

G-TERM SAVINGS (25%)		SPENDING (40%)		Total All Balances
	Cost:			
nsaction	Balance	Transaction	Balance	

MONEY PLANNER FOR KIDS

Ages: 9 and up

Spiritual Building Block: Contentment

You can learn about contentment in the following ways:

THINK ABOUT IT:

Before you go shopping for something you need (or want), plan how much money to spend and what things you'll be looking for (size, price, special features, color, etc.). In the store, take enough time to find the items that match what you had set out to find. Think about how and why some options won't work and some will.

TALK ABOUT IT:

Next time you go shopping, listen for things said by other shoppers that indicate they're trying to shop by a list or that they want to spend only a certain amount of money. Also notice when other people are saying things that indicate they're content or discontent with what is being purchased.

TRY IT:

Decide on a set amount of money to spend for your friend's birthday or Christmas present, think about the kinds of things the person likes that could be purchased for that amount of money, then head to a discount shopping store. Look at several different gift options and select an item or items that will fit within the budget.